1st Workshop on Open Community-Driven Machine Translation 2023

Tampere, Finland
15 June 2023

Editors:

Miquel Espla-Gomis
Mikel L. Forcada
Taja Kuzman
Nikola Ljubesic
Rik van Noord
Gema Ramirez-Sanchez
Jorg Tiedemann
Antonio Toral

ISBN: 978-1-7138-8995-3

Printed from e-media with permission by:

Curran Associates, Inc.
57 Morehouse Lane
Red Hook, NY 12571

Some format issues inherent in the e-media version may also appear in this print version.

Printed with permission by Curran Associates, Inc. (2024)

For permission requests, please contact the Association for Computational Linguistics at the address below.

Association for Computational Linguistics
209 N. Eighth Street
Stroudsburg, Pennsylvania 18360

Phone: 1-570-476-8006
Fax: 1-570-476-0860

acl@aclweb.org

Additional copies of this publication are available from:

Curran Associates, Inc.
57 Morehouse Lane
Red Hook, NY 12571 USA
Phone: 845-758-0400
Fax: 845-758-2633
Email: curran@proceedings.com
Web: www.proceedings.com

crowdMT.

Proceedings of the

1st Workshop on Open Community-Driven Machine Translation

June 15 2023
Tampere, Finland

Edited by

Miquel Esplà-Gomis (Universitat d'Alacant, Spain), Mikel L. Forcada (Universitat d'Alacant, Spain), Taja Kuzman (Jožef Stefan Institute, Slovenia), Nikola Ljubešić (University of Ljubljana, Slovenia), Rik van Noord (University of Groningen, The Netherlands), Gema Ramírez-Sánchez (Prompsit Language Engineering, Spain), Jörg Tiedemann (University of Helsinki, Finland), Antonio Toral (University of Groningen, The Netherlands)

Organised by

macocu

Contents

Organising committee

Miquel Esplà-Gomis (Universitat d'Alacant, Spain)

Mikel L. Forcada (Universitat d'Alacant, Spain)

Taja Kuzman (Jožef Stefan Institute, Slovenia)

Nikola Ljubešić (University of Ljubljana, Slovenia)

Rik van Noord (University of Groningen, The Netherlands)

Gema Ramírez-Sánchez (Prompsit Language Engineering, Spain)

Jörg Tiedemann (University of Helsinki, Finland)

Antonio Toral (University of Groningen, The Netherlands)

Programme Committee

Miquel Esplà Gomis (Universitat d'Alacant, Spain) Mikel L. Forcada (Universitat d'Alacant, Spain) Taja Kuzman (Jožef Stefan Institute, Slovenia) Nikola Ljubešić (Jožef Stefan Institute, Slovenia) Rik van Noord (University of Groningen, The Netherlands) Juan Antonio Pérez-Ortiz (Universitat d'Alacant, Spain) Gema Ramírez Sánchez (Prompsit Language Engineering, Spain) Peter Rupnik (Jožef Stefan Institute, Slovenia) Felipe Sánchez-Martínez (Universitat d'Alacant, Spain Víctor Manuel Sánchez-Cartagena (Universitat d'Alacant, Spain) Jörg Tiedemann (University of Helsinki, Finland) Antonio Toral (University of Groningen, The Netherlands) Jaume Zaragoza-Bernabeu (Prompsit Language Engineering, Spain)

Invited Speeches

Apertium: empowering vulnerable language communities through free/open source rule-based machine translation

Mikel L. Forcada, Universitat d'Alacant (Alacant, Spain) and Prompsit Language Engineering (Elx, Spain)

Language technologies, including machine translation, are crucial in our multilingual world, particularly since a growing fraction of communication takes place online. For many languages, reasonably useful machine translation does not yet exist, or if there is, it is often in the hands of one or a few companies —with honourable exceptions. In the age of neural machine translation and deep learning, a concentration of translation power occurs: only a few privileged companies (a) possess the necessary resources to collect and curate bilingual corpora which they do not publish, (b) are able to train and execute neural machine translation models which they usually do not publish, and (c) do so on massive computers that only they can afford, generating large amounts of greenhouse gases and heat and leaving behind the waste generated when building their computing facilities. This generates a kind of technological language injustice through dynamics of technological disempowerment in the communities of the affected languages. As a result, speakers in technology-deprived or dependent communities experience an incomplete citizenship, as citizenship is built and articulated through communication. Apertium, a free/open-source rule-based machine translation platform, was born in 2005 when statistical machine translation, the precursor of neural machine translation, was blooming. Apertium was originally designed to deal with closely related languages such as Spanish and Catalan, but the free/open-source licensing attracted a community that started to create systems for other language pairs, encoding in open dictionaries and rules explicit knowledge about their languages, knowledge that can be used to create new machine translation systems or other language technologies. In this talk, I will argue in favour of a free/open-source incarnation of such a vintage but frugal and sustainable technology as rule-based machine translation as a way for vulnerable language communities to technologically empower themselves.

Machine Translation at Wikipedia

Santhosh Thottingal and Niklas Laxström, Language team, Wikimedia Foundation

Wikipedia, the multilingual encyclopedia available in over 320 languages, uses machine translation technology primarily for article translation. The translation process involves an integrated tool that utilizes various machine translation services to provide initial translations, which are then refined by editors before publication. To date, approximately 1.5 million articles have been translated. This presentation aims to introduce a human-in-the-loop product design, highlighting the provision of high-quality rich text translations through text-only machine translation, coupled with manual curation facilitated by human edits. Additionally, we will share insights and analytics pertaining to translation quality and translators. The discussion will encompass the machine translation engines employed, ranging from free and open-source systems to self-hosted services and external paid APIs. Lastly, we will present the optimization techniques employed to scale machine translation models in order to meet the performance requirements of Wikipedia.

Full papers

Training and integration of neural machine translation with MTUOC

Antoni Oliver, Sergi Álvarez
Universitat Oberta de Catalunya (UOC)
{aoliverg,salvarezvid}@uoc.edu

Abstract

In this paper the goals and main objectives of the project MTUOC are presented. This project aims to ease the process of training and integrating neural machine translation (NMT) systems into professional translation environments. The MTUOC project distributes a series of auxiliary tools that allow to perform parallel corpus compilation and preprocessing, as well as the training of NMT systems. The project also distributes a server that implements most of the communication protocols used in computer assisted translation tools.

1 Introduction

1.1 The MTUOC project

MTUOC is a project that is being developed in the Arts and Humanities Department of the Universitat Oberta de Catalunya (UOC). The main objective of the project is to facilitate the training, use and integration of neural machine translation systems. It also provides tools for training statistical systems. Most of the software needed to train such systems is distributed in the form of complete toolkits under permissive free licenses. This makes, in principle, all this technology freely available to any professional, company or institution. However, the use of these *toolkits* brings with it a number of problems:

- *Technical skills*: A relatively high level of computer literacy is required to use these programmes. Knowledge of programming languages (e.g. Python) or scripting (e.g. Bash) is required. On the other hand, the documentation of these tools is not always sufficiently detailed and not always properly updated. This means that a lot of time is wasted in trial and error processes until the tools can be used effectively.

- *Integration*: The resulting translation engines cannot be easily integrated into existing professional translation workflows. Most tools provide access through some kind of API, usually in a server-client configuration. Some CAT tools provide access to some translation systems, but not all CAT tool - translation system combinations are available.

- *Hardware*: some high hardware requirements are necessary, especially for training systems. To train statistical systems, a lot of RAM is necessary. To train neural systems, one or more powerful GPUs (Graphical Processing Units) are essential.

The MTUOC project offers solutions for the first two problems. Regarding the *technical skills* it provides a number of easy-to-use Python and Bash scripts for corpus pre-processing and system training. All these scripts are well documented and can be easily adapted to specific needs. Regarding *integration* issues, a fully configurable server is provided that supports many communication protocols. This ensures compatibility with numerous CAT tools. For example, the server can use a neural engine based on Marian, but behave as a Moses server, so it can be directly integrated with OmegaT[1], a very popular free CAT tool. The project also provides a translation client that can

[1] https://omegat.org/

Esplà-Gomis, Forcada, Kuzman, Ljubešić, van Noord, Ramírez-Sánchez, Tiedemann, Toral (eds.)
Proceedings of the 1st Workshop on Open Community-Driven Machine Translation, p. 5–13
Tampere, Finland, June 2023.

translate text and files in a variety of formats, including XLIFF. The client can also generate translation memories in TMX with the content of the machine translation, which facilitates integration into almost all CAT tools. Finally, with reference to the *hardware* problem, it should be noted that the computing requirements for training are much higher than for translation with already trained systems. Once a system is trained, it can be used for translation on any average consumer computer. In this way, many potential users can benefit from the various free engines distributed in the MTUOC project. To train customised systems, powerful GPU units are required. It is possible to purchase these units at affordable prices and install them in consumer computers. In addition, the UOC offers the possibility to establish technology transfer agreements for the training of customised systems at very competitive prices. This service is free of charge for NGOs. Since all the components of the MTUOC project are distributed under free license, any institution or company can offer customised training services using our components.

1.2 MT toolkits

As already mentioned, the MTUOC project provides auxiliary tools to work with the main neural (and statistical) machine translation *toolkits*. Although in principle the components can be adapted to work with any *toolkit*, the following have been considered and verified:

- Moses[2] (Koehn et al., 2007): is a *toolkit* for statistical MT systems training. Some of its pre-processing tools (such as tokenizers and truecasers) are still used for training neural engines.
- Marian[3] (Junczys-Dowmunt et al., 2018): is a toolkit for neural MT systems training. It is developed in C++ so it is very fast and efficient.
- OpenNMT[4] (Klein et al., 2017): it is also a *toolkit* for neural MT systems training. Two implementations are available: one based on Python and PyTorch (OpenNMT-py) and one based on TensorFlow (OpenNMT-tf). It includes a number of sub-projects as CTranslate2[5], a fast inference engine for models trained with OpenNMT, and Tokenizer, a tokenisation library with APIs for C++ and Python.
- ModernMT[6] (Bertoldi et al., 2018): until version 2.5 it provided the possibility of training both statistical and neural engines, but later versions only allow training of neural engines. It stands out for its ease of training and for providing adaptive machine translation. In this way, the translation provided will depend on the context in which the sentence to be translated is found.

1.3 Similar projects

There are a number of projects similar to MTUOC that also distribute neural engines and auxiliary programs that can be run on personal computers. One notable project is OpusMT[7]. (Tiedemann and Thottingal, 2020), which provides around 1,000 ready-to-run neural machine translation models to run on a machine translation server. Specifically, this project provides:

- Translation engines based on Marian-NMT.
- The engines are trained with corpora from the Opus-MT-Train collection[8]
- The provided scripts can be used to train your own systems.
- SentencePiece (Kudo and Richardson, 2018) is used in most engines for the calculation of subword units.
- Most engines have been trained using *guided alignment* based on word-level alignment using eflomal[9] (Östling, 2016).
- The related project Opus-Translator[10] provides a server that can run the trained engines.
- The related project OPUS-CAT[11] implements a plug-in for Trados Studio, a computer-

[2] `http://www.statmt.org/moses/`
[3] `https://marian-nmt.github.io/`
[4] `https://opennmt.net/`
[5] `https://github.com/OpenNMT/CTranslate2`
[6] `https://github.com/modernmt/modernmt`
[7] `https://github.com/Helsinki-NLP/Opus-MT`
[8] `https://github.com/Helsinki-NLP/Opus-MT-train`
[9] `https://github.com/robertostling/eflomal`
[10] `https://github.com/Helsinki-NLP/OPUS-translator`
[11] `https://github.com/Helsinki-NLP/OPUS-CAT`

assisted translation tool widely used in professional environments.

The models trained in the Opus-MT project are also distributed in HuggingFace[12] (Wolf et al., 2019), further facilitating the use of these engines.

Softcatalà[13] is a non-profit association whose main objective is to promote the use of the Catalan language in computing, Internet and new technologies. This association leads numerous projects for the localisation of free software projects into Catalan. To facilitate this localisation, they use machine translation engines and for some years now they have been training their own neural engines, which they distribute under a free licence (Irigoyen et al., 2020). At the time of writing, the following engines including Catalan were offered with the following languages in the two directions: German, Spanish, French, Dutch, Italian, Portuguese and Spanish. The models are trained with OpenNMT and can be used with the components of this toolkit and also with CTranslate2. In addition Softcatalà provides a set of tools to use the trained models:

- A tool for processing texts in various formats into the OpenNMT input text format.
- A server program that provides an API to translate through a web service.
- Tools to directly translate text files or files in PO format.

2 Components of the MTUOC project

The MTUOC project offers a series of programs and scripts covering all steps from the creation of parallel corpora, their cleaning and corpus combination, to a program that allows to evaluate the trained systems using the most common automatic metrics. It also offers a series of scripts for corpus preparation and pre-processing and training using the toolkits presented in section 1.2. It also provides a complete server that is able to communicate with the servers provided by the main toolkits and to communicate with the client using a large number of protocols. The programs and scripts of the MTUOC project are programmed in Python version 3 or are Bash scripts. All components can be downloaded from the project's Github page and are distributed under a free licence. In this section we present a brief description of each of these components.

2.1 Programs for the creation of parallel corpora

Training neural machine translation systems requires large and good quality parallel corpora. While there are methods and toolkits for unsupervised training from monolingual corpora, supervised systems using parallel corpora achieve much higher levels of quality. Systems can be trained with parallel corpora available in a number of repositories, including OPUS[14] (Tiedemann, 2012). However, in professional environments it is common to have large amounts of parallel texts for specific topics and clients, usually in some translation memory format (TMX, SDLTM, etc.) or in the form of completed translation projects (often in the standard XLIFF format). To take advantage of these resources in system training, the MTUOC project provides a number of utilities:

- `TMXdetectlanguages`: detects the language codes present in a given TMX file or in all TMX files in a given directory.
- `TMX2tabtxt`: converts a TMX file or all TMX files in a given directory to tabular text. It supports more than one possible language code for the source language and the target language.
- `sdltm2tabtxt`: converts one SDL-Trados (SDLTM) memory or all memories in a given directory to tabular text format.
- `XLIFF2tabtxt`: converts a translation project interchange file (XLIFF) or all files in a given directory to tabular text format.

Another very common situation in professional environments is to have a large set of original and translated documents of a given subject and client, although the corresponding translation memories are not available. The MTUOC project provides a series of auxiliary tools that facilitate the alignment of these documents with hunalign[15] (Varga et al., 2007):

- a program for segmenting using SRX files (*Segmentation Rules eXchange*). It allows to

[12] `https://huggingface.co/`
[13] `https://www.softcatala.org/`
[14] `https://opus.nlpl.eu/`
[15] `https://github.com/danielvarga/hunalign`

segment a single file or all files in a directory. The program can include the paragraph marks (<p>) required by hunalign.

- a series of bilingual dictionaries for various language pairs in the format required by hunalign. These dictionaries have been created from the transfer dictionaries of the Apertium machine translation system Apertium[16] (Forcada et al., 2011).

- A program for creating the alignment script with hunalign to speed up the alignment of large numbers of documents.

- A program to select aligned segments above a certain value of the confidence index provided by hunalign.

When the files to align are parallel, that is, there is a quite good correspondence between the source and target documents, using hunalign we can get very accurate alignments. It can handle missing segments in one of the languages, and it can also handle different relations between source and target segments (1 to many and many to one).

In some cases, we can get a set of documents in the source language and a set in the target language. These documents can be translation equivalents but we don't know which document is the translation, as the names doesn't' match. The documents can talk about similar concept but they are different, and some parallel segments might exists. In these cases, techniques for mining parallel segments in comparable corpora (Schwenk, 2018) may be very productive. The MTUOC project includes a program that can perform this mining using SBERT (Reimers and Gurevych, 2019). The program provides you with parallel segments sorted by a confidence score. A visual inspection of the results is usual enough to select the lower score limit and reject parallel segments with a lower score.

2.2 Parallel corpus cleaning program

When obtaining or creating a parallel corpus, it is useful to clean up the corpus. MTUOC provides a parallel corpus cleaning program (`MTUOC_clean_parallel_corpus.py`) that can perform the following actions:

[16] `https://www.apertium.org/`

- Replace the typographical apostrophe with the standard apostrophe (`norm_apostrophe`).

- Remove HMTL and XML tags (`remove tags`).

- Replace HTML/XML entities with their corresponding characters (`unescape_html`).

- Remove parallel segments with empty segments (`remove empty`).

- Remove segments that are too short by setting a minimum number of characters (`remove_short`).

- Remove segments where the segment in the source language and the segment in the target language are the same (`remove_equal`).

- Remove the segments in which the percentage of numbers in either language is higher than a certain value (`remove_NUMPC`).

- If you want to preprocess to train Moses systems, replace the characters [and | in the corpus by their corresponding HMTL entities (`escapeforMoses`).

- Remove segments containing the specified elements from a file (`stringFromFile`).

- Remove segments that match at some point the regular expressions indicated in a file (`regexFromFile`).

- Check that the language of the source segment is correct (`vSL`).

- Check that the language of the target segment is correct (`vSL`).

- Check that the language of the target segment is not a certain language (`vNOTL`).

- The number of languages detected by the automatic language detection algorithm can be limited by using the `vSetLanguages` option.

- Remove segments written in upper case (`noUPPER`).

2.3 Parallel corpora rescoring

Once we have cleaned the corpus, we have a set of segment pairs that do not have any of the selected problems. Anyway, both segments in the segment pair can be clean, but they may not be translation equivalents. It is possible to calculate a score that provides an idea of the translation equivalence between the source and target segments in the segment pair. This can be achieved calculating the sentence embedding of the source and target segment using a multilingual model, and calculating a distance measure, as the cosine distance, for example.

The toolkit provides a program that performs two actions:

- Language detection of the source and target segments, using fasttext. This tool offers two interesting features: it returns the detected language along with a detection confidence score and users can easily train their own language detection models.
- Scoring all the segments with the cosine distance of the sentence embedding representation calculated using a multilingual model, LaBSE (Feng et al., 2022) by default.

After the scoring process is completed, we use a companion program to select the parallel segments matching a series of conditions: languages detected and language detection confidence score; and a minimum confidence score based on the cosine distance.

2.4 Parallel corpus combination program

Another common situation in professional environments is to have a large number of translation memories and original and translated texts which, once processed with the programs described in section 2.1, generate a parallel corpus of insufficient size for system training. The MTUOC project provides a series of programs to select from a parallel corpus the segments most similar to those of another parallel corpus. For example, we have a parallel corpus A of the pair L1 - L2 but it is not large enough to train a system. We also have a much larger corpus B for the same language pair. We are interested in selecting from corpus B the segments that are most similar to those of corpus A. The program calculates the L1 language model from corpus A and from this language model it selects the most similar segments from corpus B (verifying the perplexity of the L1 segments of corpus B with respect to the language model). The program also divides the A+B corpus into three parts:

- training (train): will contain segments from A and B.
- validation (val): will contain only segments from A.
- evaluation (eval): will contain only segments from A.

In this way, corpus B extends only the training corpus, as the validation is carried out exclusively with segments of corpus A.

The same program can be used in the case we only have a monolingual corpus A and a parallel corpus B. We can select the most similar parallel segments from B using the corpus A. In this case, when dividing the resulting corpus into training, validation and evaluation, all these sets will contain only segments from corpus B.

2.5 Script for the preparation of parallel corpora

MTUOC distributes all the necessary components to prepare the parallel corpus for further preprocessing. We have made a distinction between these two phases, preparation and preprocessing, since the preparation steps are (or at least can be) common for the training of statistical and neural systems. In contrast, the preprocessing step will be different. The components for corpus preparation are:

- Tokenisers for the following languages: Aragonese (arg), Asturian (ast), Catalan (cat), German (deu), English (eng), French (fra), Galician (gal), Italian (ita), japanese (jap), Portuguese (por), Russian (rus), Sardinian (srd), Spanish (spa) and Chinese (zho). A generic tokeniser (gen) is also distributed which can be used for other languages. In addition, a pseudo-tokeniser is distributed for Chinese (zho-pseudo) which simply separates all characters in the file by whitespace and another Chinese tokeniser based on the jieba footnote library[17] (zho_jieba). These tokenisers have different modes of operation and can

[17] https://github.com/fxsjy/jieba

represent tokens with either *joiners* or *splitters* to facilitate subsequent detokenisation. Tokenisers also function as detokenisers. Tokenisers give the option to separate digits from numerical expressions, a common practice in neural engine training. New language-specific tokenisers for other languages will be added in the future.

- Truecasers, both the training program and the program that carries out the truecasing process. The truecaser can be trained with a corpus and a dictionary of language forms.
- Programs to replace emails and URLs with configurable codes.
- Program for splitting the corpus into fragments of different number of segments. It is useful to divide the corpus into training, validation and evaluation fragments.

All these steps can be performed with a single program that is fully configurable by means of a yaml configuration file, which can be easily edited in any text editor.

2.6 Scripts for the preprocessment of parallel corpora

In this step we perform a series of operations that depend on the type of engine we want to train. Three different programs are provided, which are configured by means of yaml files.

- For statistical engines, the steps of replacing numerical expressions with codes are performed and the characters [and | are replaced by their corresponding entities.
- For neural engines using BPE (Byte Pair Encoding) (Sennrich et al., 2016) for subword calculation using the subword-nmt algorithm[18].
- For neural engines using SentencePiece[19] (Kudo and Richardson, 2018) for subword computation.

2.7 Training scripts

Scripts for training translation systems are provided for several toolkits, namely

- Moses: scripts are provided to perform all the training in one step or to perform the different steps individually: training (of the language and translation model), SALM (Suffix Array tool kit for empirical Language Manipulations), optimisation and binarisation.
- Marian: scripts for s2s and transformer systems.
- OpenNMT: scripts for transformer type systems.

2.8 MTUOC server

The models we train, whether statistical with Moses or neural with Marian or OpenNMT, can be implemented in a program that works as a translation server, that is, as a program that waits to receive segments to be translated and returns these translated segments. Figure 1 shows the operation scheme of the client-server configuration. The client can be the MTUOC-Translator (see section 2.9) or a CAT tool. This client program sends the segments to the MTUOC server. The segments can be sent and received in different protocols, which allows this machine translation system to be compatible with various computer-assisted translation tools. Specifically, it can use the following protocols:

- MTUOC: a simple protocol specific to the project. We have developed a plug-in for Trados Studio 2019, 2021 and 2022.[20]
- Moses: the same protocol used by the server provided by this toolkit. It can be used, for example, with OmegaT and Trados Studio 2017 and 2019.
- ModernMT: the same protocol as the server provided by this toolkit. It can be used, for example, with Okapi tools[21] (Tikal and Rainbow).
- OpenNMT: the same protocol as the server provide by this toolkit.
- NMTWizard: the same protocol used by this server.[22].

[18] https://github.com/rsennrich/subword-nmt

[19] https://github.com/google/sentencepiece

[20] https://github.com/aoliverg/MTUOC-Trados-plugin

[21] https://okapiframework.org/

[22] https://github.com/OpenNMT/nmt-wizard

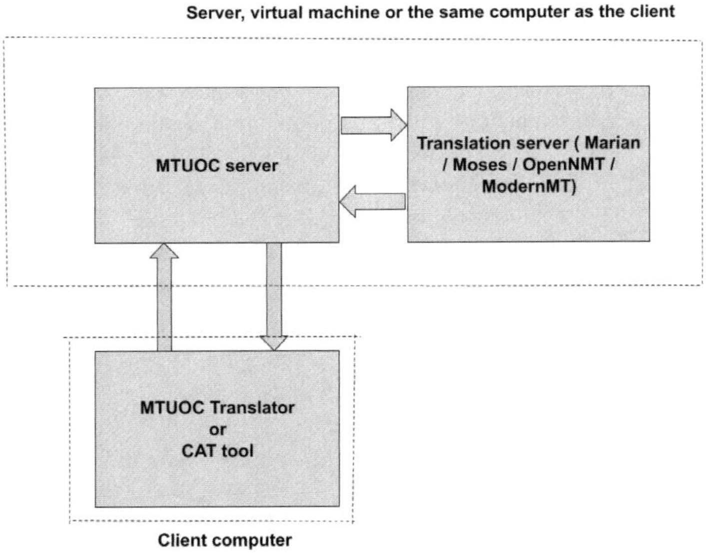

Figure 1: Client-Server configuration in MTUOC engines

The client sends the segment as it is, and the MTUOC server preprocesses it (e.g. tokenises, truecases and SentencePiece) and sends it to the appropriate translation server (e.g. marian-server). When the MTUOC server receives the translated segment it post-processes it (e.g. detokenises, detruecases and undoes the SentencePiece subword) and sends it back to the client program.

Do not confuse the protocol that the MTUOC server will use with the translation system it will use. For example, we may have a neural engine trained with Marian but we want to use it with a tool that is only compatible with the Moses server protocol. In this case we can run the MTUOC server in Moses mode and it will be compatible with the desired tool, but it will actually be translating with a Marian neural engine.

MTUOC-server can be run in personal computers or in physical or virtual servers. Running the server in your own computer or server ensures you full confidentiality, as no information goes out from your premises. No GPU is required to run the server, but using GPUs will speed up scientifically the translation speed. Having your own engines integrated in MTUOC-server allows you to run as much instances as necessary in case of very heavy use. For very heavy use scenarios, a wsgi server such as gunicorn[23] can be used along with MTUOC-server.

[23]`https://gunicorn.org/`

2.9 MTUOC Translator

The MTUOC project provides a client program with a simple user interface that allows to translate segments and files in different formats. It also provides a version without graphical interface that is useful in the evaluation process of trained engines.

2.10 Tag processing in MTUOC

The MTUOC server includes an automatic XML/HTML tag retrieval algorithm. The training of the engines is carried out with corpora in which all tags have been removed and the translation is carried out with untagged segments. If the segment to be translated contains tags, these are removed. Once the segment has been translated, the tags are retrieved from the original segment with tags, from the untagged translation and from the alignment information provided by the translation engine. Statistical engines trained with Moses are able to return reliable alignment information. Neural engines, especially if they are of the transformer type, do not return reliable alignment if they are not trained with *guided alignment*. If trained with *guided alignment* they are able to return quite accurate alignment information, but this information will be relative to the sub-words.

The tag retrieval algorithm is able to retrieve tags even if subword-based information is available.

2.11 Evaluation program

The project distributes an evaluation program that provides several automatic evaluation metrics: BLEU (Papineni et al., 2002), NIST (Doddington, 2002), WER (Word Error Rate) (Nießen et al., 2000), %Ed. dist., TER (Translation Error Rate) (Klakow and Peters, 2002) and COMET[24] (Reimers and Gurevych, 2019).

To facilitate the use of this program, it is provided in two versions: one with a graphical user interface and one to be used from the terminal. The program calculates global values and it can also calculate detailed values by segment.

3 Free MT engines

The MTUOC project provides a growing number of freely downloadable MT engines. Most of the engines are based on Marian with a transformer configuration and guided-alignment. At the time of writing this paper, the following engines were available:

- General language: spa↔cat, eng↔spa, eng↔cat, fra↔spa, fra↔cat, rus↔spa, rus ↔cat
- International relations (using UNPC corpus): ara↔spa, eng ↔spa, fra ↔spa, rus ↔spa, zho ↔spa. Catalan version with synthetic corpora through Spanish using Apertium: ara↔cat, eng ↔cat, fra ↔cat, rus ↔cat, zho ↔cat.
- Patents (using EuroPat corpus): eng ↔spa, eng ↔fra, eng ↔deu.
- Legislation (using the DOGC corpus): cat ↔spa

  The complete and up-to-date list of MT engines can be seen in the MTUOC project wiki.[25]

4 Conclusions and future work

In this paper we have presented the MTUOC project, aiming to make the process of training and integrating NMT systems easier. With the components of this project, any professional or translation company will be able to use their own MT systems. One of the goals of the project is to make the developed tools usable for most users, regardless of their technical skills. We are now working on converting the scripts into programs with GUI interfaces to make them even easier to use.

This set of tools is being actively used in teaching activities at the bachelor and master levels at the UOC, and students with no previous knowledge of the use of terminal and scripts are able to perform all the processes involved in the training of statistical and neural systems. The tools are also being used in production environments, where custom NMT systems have been trained and used in translation projects.

In the future we plan to train and make freely available more NMT systems. We also want to offer NMT systems for low resourced language pairs, starting for some Romance languages in Spain: Asturian, Aragonses and Aranese.

[24] `https://unbabel.github.io/COMET/html/index.html`

[25] `https://github.com/aoliverg/MTUOC-project/wiki`

Acknowledgments

This work is partially supported by the project *TAN-IBE: Neural Machine Translation for the romance languages of the Iberian Peninsula*, founded by the Spanish Ministry of Science and Innovation Proyectos de generación de conocimiento 2021. Reference: PID2021-124663OB-I00.

References

Bertoldi, Nicola, Davide Caroselli, and Marcello Federico. 2018. The ModernMT project. In *Proceedings of the 21st Annual Conference of the European Association for Machine Translation.*

Doddington, George. 2002. Automatic Evaluation of Machine Translation Quality Using N-gram Co-occurrence Statistics. *Proceedings of the Second International Conference on Human Language Technology Research*, pages 138–145.

Feng, Fangxiaoyu, Yinfei Yang, Daniel Cer, Naveen Arivazhagan, and Wei Wang. 2022. Language-agnostic bert sentence embedding. In *Proceedings of the 60th Annual Meeting of the Association for Computational Linguistics (Volume 1: Long Papers)*, pages 878–891.

Forcada, Mikel L, Mireia Ginestí-Rosell, Jacob Nordfalk, Jim O'Regan, Sergio Ortiz-Rojas, Juan Antonio Pérez-Ortiz, Felipe Sánchez-Martínez, Gema Ramírez-Sánchez, and Francis M Tyers. 2011. Apertium: a free/open-source platform for rule-based machine translation. *Machine translation*, 25(2):127–144.

Irigoyen, Marc Riera, Xavier Ivars Ribes, Pere Orga Esteve, Joan Montané Camacho, Jordi Mas Hernández, and Artur Vicedo Cremades. 2020. Softcatalà: nous reptes per garantir la vitalitat del català a les tecnologies. *Revista de Llengua i Dret*, (73):146–153.

Junczys-Dowmunt, Marcin, Roman Grundkiewicz, Tomasz Dwojak, Hieu Hoang, Kenneth Heafield, Tom Neckermann, Frank Seide, Ulrich Germann, Alham Fikri Aji, Nikolay Bogoychev, André F. T. Martins, and Alexandra Birch. 2018. Marian: Fast neural machine translation in C++. In *Proceedings of ACL 2018, System Demonstrations*, pages 116–121, Melbourne, Australia, July. Association for Computational Linguistics.

Klakow, Dietrich and Jochen Peters. 2002. Testing the correlation of word error rate and perplexity. *Speech Communication*, 38(1-2):19–28.

Klein, Guillaume, Yoon Kim, Yuntian Deng, Jean Senellart, and Alexander M. Rush. 2017. OpenNMT: Open-source toolkit for neural machine translation. In *Proceedings of ACL 2017, System Demonstrations*, page 67–72.

Koehn, Philipp, Hieu Hoang, Alexandra Birch, Chris Callison-Burch, Marcello Federico, Nicola Bertoldi, Brooke Cowan, Wade Shen, Christine Moran, Richard Zens, et al. 2007. Moses: Open source toolkit for statistical machine translation. In *Proceedings of the 45th annual meeting of the association for computational linguistics companion volume proceedings of the demo and poster sessions*, pages 177–180.

Kudo, Taku and John Richardson. 2018. Sentencepiece: A simple and language independent subword tokenizer and detokenizer for neural text processing. In *Proceedings of the 2018 Conference on Empirical Methods in Natural Language Processing: System Demonstrations*, pages 66–71.

Nießen, Sonja, Franz Josef Och, Gregor Leusch, Hermann Ney, et al. 2000. An evaluation tool for machine translation: Fast evaluation for MT research. In *Proceedings of the LREC Conference Athens, Greece, 2000*. Citeseer.

Östling, Robert. 2016. Efficient word alignment with markov chain monte carlo. *The Prague Bulletin of Mathematical Linguistics*, (106):125–146.

Papineni, Kishore, Salim Roukos, Todd Ward, and Wj Zhu. 2002. BLEU: a method for automatic evaluation of machine translation. *Proceedings of the 40th Annual Meeting of the Association for Computational Linguistics*, pages 311–318.

Reimers, Nils and Iryna Gurevych. 2019. Sentence-bert: Sentence embeddings using siamese bert-networks. In *Proceedings of the 2019 Conference on Empirical Methods in Natural Language Processing*. Association for Computational Linguistics, 11.

Schwenk, Holger. 2018. Filtering and mining parallel data in a joint multilingual space. In *Proceedings of the 56th Annual Meeting of the Association for Computational Linguistics (Volume 2: Short Papers)*, pages 228–234.

Sennrich, Rico, Barry Haddow, and Alexandra Birch. 2016. Neural machine translation of rare words with subword units. In *Proceedings of the 54th Annual Meeting of the Association for Computational Linguistics (Volume 1: Long Papers)*, pages 1715–1725.

Tiedemann, Jörg and Santhosh Thottingal. 2020. OPUS-MT — Building open translation services for the World. In *Proceedings of the 22nd Annual Conferenec of the European Association for Machine Translation (EAMT)*, Lisbon, Portugal.

Tiedemann, Jörg. 2012. Parallel data, tools and interfaces in opus. In *Lrec*, volume 2012, pages 2214–2218.

Varga, Dániel, Péter Halácsy, András Kornai, Viktor Nagy, László Németh, and Viktor Trón. 2007. Parallel corpora for medium density languages. In *Recent Advances in Natural Language Processing IV*, pages 247–258. John Benjamins.

Wolf, Thomas, Lysandre Debut, Victor Sanh, Julien Chaumond, Clement Delangue, Anthony Moi, Pierric Cistac, Tim Rault, Rémi Louf, Morgan Funtowicz, et al. 2019. Huggingface's transformers: State-of-the-art natural language processing. *arXiv preprint arXiv:1910.03771*.

Design of an Open-Source Architecture for Neural Machine Translation

Séamus Lankford
ADAPT Centre,
MTU, Cork, Ireland
seamus.lankford@mtu.ie

Haithem Afli
ADAPT Centre,
MTU, Cork, Ireland
haithem.afli@mtu.ie

Andy Way
ADAPT Centre,
DCU, Dublin, Ireland
andy.way@dcu.ie

Abstract

adaptNMT is an open-source application that offers a streamlined approach to the development and deployment of Recurrent Neural Networks and Transformer models. This application is built upon the widely-adopted OpenNMT ecosystem, and is particularly useful for new entrants to the field, as it simplifies the setup of the development environment and creation of train, validation, and test splits. The application offers a graphing feature that illustrates the progress of model training, and employs SentencePiece for creating subword segmentation models. Furthermore, the application provides an intuitive user interface that facilitates hyperparameter customization. Notably, a single-click model development approach has been implemented, and models developed by adaptNMT can be evaluated using a range of metrics. To encourage eco-friendly research, adaptNMT incorporates a green report that flags the power consumption and $kgCO_2$ emissions generated during model development. The application is freely available.[1]

1 Credits

This research is supported by Science Foundation Ireland through the ADAPT Centre (Grant 13/RC/2106) (www.adaptcentre.ie) at Dublin City University. This research was also funded by the Munster Technological University.

[1] http://github.com/adaptNMT

2 Introduction

Explainable Artificial Intelligence (XAI) (Arrieta et al., 2020) aims to ensure that the outcomes of AI solutions are easily comprehensible to humans. In light of this goal, adaptNMT has been developed to provide users with a form of Explainable Neural Machine Translation (XNMT). The typical NMT process comprises several independent stages, including setting up the environment, preparing the dataset, training subword models, parameterizing and training the main models, evaluating and deploying them. By adopting a modular approach, this framework has established an effective NMT model development process that caters to both technical and non-technical practitioners in the field. To address the environmental impact of building and running large AI models (Henderson et al., 2020; Jooste et al., 2022b), we have also produced a "green report" that calculates carbon emissions. While primarily intended as an information aid, this report will hopefully encourage the development of reusable and sustainable models.

This research endeavors to create models and applications that address the challenges of language technology, which will be particularly beneficial for those new to the field of Machine Translation (MT) and those seeking to learn more about NMT.

The application is built on OpenNMT[2] (Klein et al., 2017) and thus inherits all of its features. Unlike many NMT toolkits, a command line interface (CLI) is not used, and the interface is designed and fully implemented in Google Colab.[3] For both educational and research purposes, a cloud-hosted solution like Colab is often more user-friendly.

[2] https://opennmt.net
[3] colab.research.google.com

Esplà-Gomis, Forcada, Kuzman, Ljubešić, van Noord, Ramírez-Sánchez, Tiedemann, Toral (eds.)
Proceedings of the 1st Workshop on Open Community-Driven Machine Translation, p. 15–20
Tampere, Finland, June 2023.

Additionally, the training of models can be monitored and controlled via a Google Colab mobile app, which is useful for long-run builds. The adaptNMT framework also includes GUI controls that allow for the customization of all crucial parameters needed for NMT model training.

The application can be run in local mode to utilize existing infrastructure or hosted mode for rapid infrastructure scaling. A deploy function is also included to allow for the immediate deployment of trained models.

This paper begins by presenting background information on NMT and NMT tools in Section 3, followed by a detailed description of the adaptNMT architecture and its key features in Section 4. The system is discussed in Section 5 before concluding with a discussion of future work in Section 6. A more in-depth system description, coupled with an empirical evaluation of models developed using the application, is outlined in a separate paper (Lankford et al., 2023a).

3 Related Work

3.1 NMT

In addition to the ongoing research dedicated to developing state-of-the-art (SOTA) NMT models, comprehensive descriptions of this technology are readily available in the literature, making it accessible to individuals who are new to the field or have limited technical expertise (Way, 2019).

NMT has benefitted from the availability of large parallel corpora, leading to the development of high-performing MT models. The field of MT has experienced significant advancements through the application of NMT, particularly after the introduction of the Transformer (Vaswani et al., 2017) architecture, which has resulted in SOTA performance across multiple language pairs (Bojar et al., 2017; Bojar et al., 2018; Lankford et al., 2021a; Lankford et al., 2021b; Lankford et al., 2022a; Lankford et al., 2022b).

3.2 NMT Tools

In essence, adaptNMT is an IPython wrapper built on OpenNMT, enabling it to benefit from OpenNMT's extensive feature set and continuous code maintenance. However, adaptNMT takes abstraction to a higher level than OpenNMT, with greater focus on usability, particularly for newcomers. As a result, adaptNMT facilitates easy and fast deployment, offering features such as more preprocessing, as well as GUI control over model creation. Moreover, it incorporates green features in line with current research efforts towards smaller models with reduced carbon footprints, making it suitable for educational and research environments alike.

Other commonly used frameworks for developing NMT systems include FAIRSEQ[4] (Ott et al., 2019), an open-source sequence modelling toolkit based on PyTorch that allows for training models for translation, summarization, and language modelling. Marian[5] (Junczys-Dowmunt et al., 2018), on the other hand, is an NMT framework based on dynamic computation graphs and developed using C++. OpenNMT is an open-source NMT framework that has been widely adopted in the research community and covers the entire MT workflow from data preparation to live inference.

4 Architecture of adaptNMT

After providing a general overview of NMT and NMT development systems, we introduce the adaptNMT tool, which enables users to configure the components of the NMT development process. The platform's system architecture is depicted in Figure 1. The tool is built as an IPython notebook and leverages the Pytorch implementation of OpenNMT for training models. Additionally, SentencePiece is used to train subword models. Using a Jupyter notebook facilitates sharing the application with other members of the MT community, and the application's setup is simplified since all necessary packages are downloaded dynamically as the application runs.

The system has two deployment options: running it locally or as a Colab instance via Google Cloud. In order to build translation models, the system requires parallel text corpora for both the source and target languages. A Tensorboard visualization allows for real-time monitoring of the model training process. At runtime, users can select to use the system for either model building or translation services, or both. Additionally, as depicted in Figure 1, the system enables the generation of an ensemble output during translation. Finally, trained models can be easily deployed to a pre-configured location.

[4] `https://github.com/facebookresearch/fairseq`

[5] `https://marian-nmt.github.io`

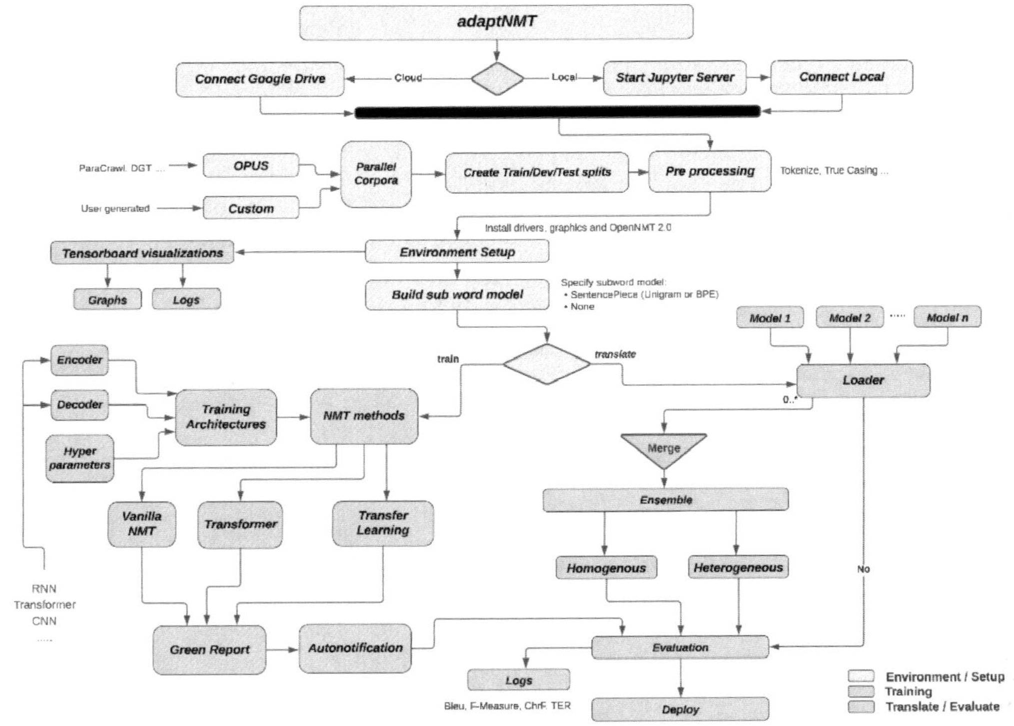

Figure 1: Proposed architecture for adaptNMT: a language-agnostic NMT development environment. The system is designed to run either in the cloud or using local infrastructure. Models are trained using parallel corpora. Visualization and extensive logging enable real-time monitoring. Models are developed using vanilla RNN-based NMT, Transformer-based approaches or transfer learning using a fine-tuning approach. Translation and evaluation can be carried out using either single models or ensembles.

4.1 adaptNMT

The application may be run as an IPython Jupyter notebook or as a Google Colab application. Given the ease of integrating large Google drive storage into Colab, the application has been used exclusively as a Google Colab application for our own experiments.

4.1.1 Initialization and logging

Initialization enables connection to Google Drive to run experiments, automatic installation of Python, OpenNMT,[6] SentencePiece,[7] Pytorch and other applications. The visualization section enables real-time graphing of model development. All log files are stored and can be viewed to inspect training convergence, the model's training and validation accuracy and changes in learning rates.

4.1.2 Modes of operation

There are two modes of operation: local or cloud. In local mode, the application is run so that models are built using the user's local GPU resources. The option to use cloud mode enables users to develop models using Google's GPU clusters. For shorter training times, the unpaid Colab option is adequate. However, for a small monthly subscription, the Google Colab Pro option is worthwhile since users have access to improved GPU and compute resources. Furthermore, using Google Cloud may be considered as the "green option" since its platform uses 100% renewables (Lacoste et al., 2019).

4.1.3 Customization of models

The system has been developed to allow users to select variations to the underlying model architecture. A vanilla RNN or Transformer approach may be selected to develop the NMT model. The customization mode enables users to specify the exact parameters required for the chosen approach. One of the features, AutoBuild, enables a user to build an NMT model in three simple steps: (i) upload source and target files, (ii) select RNN or Transformer, and (iii) click AutoBuild.

[6] https://opennmt.net

[7] https://github.com/google/sentencepiece

4.1.4 Use of subword segmentation

In the NMT development process, users can specify the type of optimizer for learning and choose from different subword models. The subword model functionality allows for the selection of a subword model type and the choice of vocabulary size, currently offering either a SentencePiece unigram or a SentencePiece BPE model.

A user may upload a dataset which includes the train, validation and test splits for both source and target languages. In cases where a user has not already created the required splits for model training, single source and target files may be uploaded. Automated splitting of the uploaded dataset into train, validation, and test files is then performed based on the user's chosen split ratio.

Given that building NMT models typically demands long training times, an automatic notification feature is incorporated that informs the user by email when model training has been completed.

4.1.5 Translation and evaluation

The application supports not only the training of models but also the translation and evaluation of model performance. For translation using pre-built models, users can specify the model name as a hyperparameter which is subsequently used to translate and evaluate the test files. The option for creating an ensemble output is also available, with users simply naming the models to be used in generating the ensemble output.

Once the system has been built, the user can select the model to be used for translating the test set. While human evaluation is often considered the most insightful approach for evaluating translation quality, it can be limited by factors such as availability, cost, and subjectivity. Thus, automatic evaluation metrics are frequently employed, particularly by developers monitoring incremental progress of systems. A further discussion on the advantages and disadvantages of human and automatic evaluation is available in the literature (Way, 2018).

Several automatic evaluation metrics provided by SacreBleu[8] (Post, 2018) are used: BLEU (Papineni et al., 2002), TER (Snover et al., 2006) and ChrF (Popović, 2015). Translation quality can also be evaluated using Meteor (Denkowski and Lavie, 2014) and F1 score (Melamed et al., 2003). Note that BLEU, ChrF, Meteor and F1 are precision-based metrics, so higher scores are better, whereas TER is an error-based metric and lower scores indicate better translation quality. Evaluation options available include standard (truecase) and lowercase BLEU scores, a sentence-level BLEU score option, ChrF1 and ChrF3.

There are three levels of logging: model development logs for graphing, training console output and experimental results. A references section outlines resources which are relevant to developing, using and understanding adaptNMT. Validation during training is currently conducted using model accuracy and perplexity (PPL).

4.2 Infrastructure

Rapid prototype development is possible through a Google Colab Pro subscription using NVIDIA Tesla P100 PCIe 16GB graphic cards and up to 27GB of memory when available.

5 Discussion

Numerous tools have been developed to assess the carbon footprint of NLP (Bannour et al., 2021). The notion of sustainable NLP has also gained momentum as an independent research track, with high-profile conferences such as the *EACL 2021 Green and Sustainable NLP* track dedicating resources to this area.[9]

Given these developments, we have incorporated a "green report" into adaptNMT that logs the $kgCO_2$ generated during model development. This aligns with the industry's increasing focus on quantifying the environmental impact of NLP. In fact, it has been demonstrated that high-performing MT systems can be developed with much lower carbon footprints, leading to significant energy cost savings for a real translation company (Jooste et al., 2022a).

The risks associated with relying on Large Language Models (LLMs) have been well-documented in the literature. The discussion surrounding these models emphasizes not only their environmental impact but also the inherent biases and dangers they pose for low-resource languages (Bender et al., 2021). It is important to note that smaller, in-domain datasets can yield high-performing NMT models, and the adaptNMT framework makes this approach easily accessible and understandable.

[8]https://github.com/mjpost/sacrebleu

[9]https://2021.eacl.org/news/green-and-sustainable-nlp

6 Conclusion and Future Work

We have introduced adaptNMT, an application that manages the entire NMT model development, evaluation, and deployment workflow.

As for future work, our development efforts will be directed towards incorporating new transfer learning methods and improving our ability to track environmental costs. We will integrate modern zero-shot and few-shot approaches, as seen in the GPT3 (Brown et al., 2020) and Facebook LASER (Artetxe and Schwenk, 2019) frameworks. While the existing adaptNMT application is focused on customizing NMT models, we will also develop a separate application, adaptLLM (Lankford et al., 2023b; Lankford et al., 2023c), for fine-tuning LLMs. In particular, adaptLLM will cater for low-resource language pairs such as NLLB (Costa-jussà et al., 2022).

The green report integrated into the application represents our first implementation of a sustainable NLP feature within adaptNMT. We plan to enhance this feature by improving the user interface and providing recommendations on how to develop greener models. As an open-source project, we invite the community to contribute new ideas and improvements to the development of this feature.

References

Arrieta, Alejandro Barredo, Natalia Díaz-Rodríguez, Javier Del Ser, Adrien Bennetot, Siham Tabik, Alberto Barbado, Salvador García, Sergio Gil-López, Daniel Molina, Richard Benjamins, et al. 2020. Explainable artificial intelligence (XAI): Concepts, taxonomies, opportunities and challenges toward responsible ai. *Information Fusion*, 58:82–115.

Artetxe, Mikel and Holger Schwenk. 2019. Massively multilingual sentence embeddings for zero-shot cross-lingual transfer and beyond. *Transactions of the Association for Computational Linguistics*, 7:597–610.

Bannour, Nesrine, Sahar Ghannay, Aurélie Névéol, and Anne-Laure Ligozat. 2021. Evaluating the carbon footprint of NLP methods: a survey and analysis of existing tools. In *Proceedings of the Second Workshop on Simple and Efficient Natural Language Processing*, pages 11–21, Virtual, November. Association for Computational Linguistics.

Bender, Emily M., Timnit Gebru, Angelina McMillan-Major, and Shmargaret Shmitchell. 2021. On the dangers of stochastic parrots: Can language models be too big? In *Proceedings of the 2021 ACM Conference on Fairness, Accountability, and Transparency*, FAccT '21, page 610–623, New York, NY, USA. Association for Computing Machinery.

Bojar, Ondřej, Rajen Chatterjee, Christian Federmann, Yvette Graham, Barry Haddow, Shujian Huang, Matthias Huck, Philipp Koehn, Qun Liu, Varvara Logacheva, Christof Monz, Matteo Negri, Matt Post, Raphael Rubino, Lucia Specia, and Marco Turchi. 2017. Findings of the 2017 conference on machine translation (WMT17). In *Proceedings of the Second Conference on Machine Translation*, pages 169–214, Copenhagen, Denmark, September. Association for Computational Linguistics.

Bojar, Ondřej, Christian Federmann, Mark Fishel, Yvette Graham, Barry Haddow, Philipp Koehn, and Christof Monz. 2018. Findings of the 2018 conference on machine translation (WMT18). In *Proceedings of the Third Conference on Machine Translation: Shared Task Papers*, pages 272–303, Belgium, Brussels, October. Association for Computational Linguistics.

Brown, Tom, Benjamin Mann, Nick Ryder, Melanie Subbiah, Jared D Kaplan, Prafulla Dhariwal, Arvind Neelakantan, Pranav Shyam, Girish Sastry, Amanda Askell, et al. 2020. Language models are few-shot learners. *Advances in neural information processing systems*, 33:1877–1901.

Costa-jussà, Marta R, James Cross, Onur Çelebi, Maha Elbayad, Kenneth Heafield, Kevin Heffernan, Elahe Kalbassi, Janice Lam, Daniel Licht, Jean Maillard, et al. 2022. No language left behind: Scaling human-centered machine translation. *arXiv preprint arXiv:2207.04672*.

Denkowski, Michael and Alon Lavie. 2014. Meteor universal: Language specific translation evaluation for any target language. In *Proceedings of the Ninth Workshop on Statistical Machine Translation*, pages 376–380, Baltimore, Maryland, USA, June. Association for Computational Linguistics.

Henderson, Peter, Jieru Hu, Joshua Romoff, Emma Brunskill, Dan Jurafsky, and Joelle Pineau. 2020. Towards the systematic reporting of the energy and carbon footprints of machine learning. *Journal of Machine Learning Research*, 21(248):1–43.

Jooste, Wandri, Rejwanul Haque, and Andy Way. 2022a. Knowledge distillation: A method for making neural machine translation more efficient. *Information*, 13(2).

Jooste, Wandri, Andy Way, Rejwanul Haque, and Riccardo Superbo. 2022b. Knowledge distillation for sustainable neural machine translation. In *Proceedings of the 15th Biennial Conference of the Association for Machine Translation in the Americas (Volume 2: Users and Providers Track and Government Track)*, pages 221–230, Orlando, USA, September. Association for Machine Translation in the Americas.

Junczys-Dowmunt, Marcin, Roman Grundkiewicz, Tomasz Dwojak, Hieu Hoang, Kenneth Heafield, Tom Neckermann, Frank Seide, Ulrich Germann, Alham Fikri Aji, Nikolay Bogoychev, André F. T. Martins, and Alexandra Birch. 2018. Marian: Fast neural machine translation in C++. In *Proceedings of ACL 2018, System Demonstrations*, pages 116–121, Melbourne, Australia, July. Association for Computational Linguistics.

Klein, Guillaume, Yoon Kim, Yuntian Deng, Jean Senellart, and Alexander Rush. 2017. OpenNMT: Open-source toolkit for neural machine translation. In *Proceedings of ACL 2017, System Demonstrations*, pages 67–72, Vancouver, Canada, July. Association for Computational Linguistics.

Lacoste, Alexandre, Alexandra Luccioni, Victor Schmidt, and Thomas Dandres. 2019. Quantifying the carbon emissions of machine learning. *arXiv preprint arXiv:1910.09700*.

Lankford, Séamus, Haithem Afli, and Andy Way. 2021a. Transformers for low-resource languages: Is féidir linn! In *Proceedings of Machine Translation Summit XVIII: Research Track*, pages 48–60.

Lankford, Séamus, Haithem Afli, and Andy Way. 2021b. Machine translation in the covid domain: an English-Irish case study for LoResMT 2021. In *Proceedings of the 4th Workshop on Technologies for MT of Low Resource Languages (LoResMT2021)*, pages 144–150, Virtual, August. Association for Machine Translation in the Americas.

Lankford, Séamus, Haithem Afli, Órla Ní Loinsigh, and Andy Way. 2022a. gaHealth: An English–Irish bilingual corpus of health data. In *Proceedings of the Thirteenth Language Resources and Evaluation Conference*, pages 6753–6758, Marseille, France, June. European Language Resources Association.

Lankford, Séamus, Haithem Afli, and Andy Way. 2022b. Human evaluation of English–Irish Transformer-Based NMT. *Information*, 13(7):309. 19pp.

Lankford, Séamus, Haithem Afli, and Andy Way. 2023a. adaptNMT: an open-source, language-agnostic development environment for neural machine translation. *Language Resources and Evaluation*.

Lankford, Séamus, Haithem Afli, and Andy Way. 2023b. adaptLLM: Fine-tuning large language models for improved machine translation. an open-source approach with NLLB and GPT-J integration. In *Journal of Artificial Intelligence Research [manuscript submitted]*, El Segundo, CA, United States. AI Access Foundation.

Lankford, Séamus, Haithem Afli, and Andy Way. 2023c. Fine-tuning LLMs using low-resource language pairs: A comparative study with loresmt2021 shared task baselines. In *Proceedings of Machine Translation Summit XIX: Research Track [manuscript submitted]*, Macau SAR, China, September 4-8. Asia-Pacific Association for Machine Translation (AAMT).

Melamed, I. Dan, Ryan Green, and Joseph P. Turian. 2003. Precision and recall of machine translation. In *Companion Volume of the Proceedings of HLT-NAACL 2003 - Short Papers*, pages 61–63, Edmonton, Canada.

Ott, Myle, Sergey Edunov, Alexei Baevski, Angela Fan, Sam Gross, Nathan Ng, David Grangier, and Michael Auli. 2019. fairseq: A fast, extensible toolkit for sequence modeling. In *Proceedings of the 2019 Conference of the North American Chapter of the Association for Computational Linguistics (Demonstrations)*, pages 48–53, Minneapolis, Minnesota, June. Association for Computational Linguistics.

Papineni, Kishore, Salim Roukos, Todd Ward, and Wei-Jing Zhu. 2002. Bleu: a method for automatic evaluation of machine translation. In *Proceedings of the 40th annual meeting of the Association for Computational Linguistics*, pages 311–318, Philadelphia, PA.

Popović, Maja. 2015. chrF: character n-gram F-score for automatic MT evaluation. In *Proceedings of the Tenth Workshop on Statistical Machine Translation*, pages 392–395, Lisbon, Portugal, September. Association for Computational Linguistics.

Post, Matt. 2018. A call for clarity in reporting BLEU scores. In *Proceedings of the Third Conference on Machine Translation: Research Papers*, pages 186–191, Brussels, Belgium, October. Association for Computational Linguistics.

Snover, Matthew, Bonnie Dorr, Rich Schwartz, Linnea Micciulla, and John Makhoul. 2006. A study of translation edit rate with targeted human annotation. In *Proceedings of the 7th Conference of the Association for Machine Translation in the Americas: Technical Papers*, pages 223–231, Cambridge, Massachusetts, USA, August 8-12. Association for Machine Translation in the Americas.

Vaswani, Ashish, Noam Shazeer, Niki Parmar, Jakob Uszkoreit, Llion Jones, Aidan N. Gomez, Łukasz Kaiser, and Illia Polosukhin. 2017. Attention is all you need. In *Proceedings of the 31st International Conference on Neural Information Processing Systems*, NIPS'17, page 6000–6010, Red Hook, NY, USA. Curran Associates Inc.

Way, Andy. 2018. Quality expectations of machine translation. In Moorkens, Joss, Sheila Castilho, Federico Gaspari, and Stephen Doherty, editors, *Translation Quality Assessment: From Principles to Practice*, pages 159–178. Springer, Cham, Switzerland.

Way, Andy. 2019. Machine translation: Where are we at today? In Angelone, Eric, Gary Massey, and Maureen Ehrensberger-Dow, editors, *The Bloomsbury Companion to Language Industry Studies*, page 311—332. Bloomsbury, London.

Creating a parallel Finnish–Easy Finnish dataset from news articles

Anna Dmitrieva
University of Helsinki
Yliopistonkatu 4, 00100 Helsinki, Finland
anna.dmitrieva@helsinki.fi

Aleksandra Konovalova
University of Turku
FI-20014 Turun yliopisto, Finland
aleksandra.a.konovalova@utu.fi

Abstract

Modern natural language processing tasks such as text simplification or summarization are typically formulated as monolingual machine translation tasks. This requires appropriate datasets to train, tune, and evaluate the models. This paper describes the creation of a parallel Finnish–Easy Finnish dataset from the Yle News archives. The dataset contains 1919 manually verified pairs of articles, each containing an article in Easy Finnish (*selkosuomi*) and a corresponding article from Standard Finnish news. Standard Finnish texts total 687555 words, and Easy Finnish texts have 106733 words. This new aligned resource was created automatically based on the Yle News archives from the Language Bank of Finland (Kielipankki) and manually checked by a human expert. The dataset is available for download from Kielipankki. This resource will allow for more effective Easy Language research and for creating applications for automatic simplification and/or summarization of Finnish texts.

1 Introduction

Easy and Plain Languages can be considered language varieties of different national languages with reduced linguistic complexity, which aim to improve the readability and comprehensibility of texts (Maaß, 2020). However, "Easy Language" is not exactly a uniform concept, but more of an umbrella term (Lindholm and Vanhatalo, 2021). Easy Language media in the Nordic countries have a long history, with the first documented signs of explicit usage of Easy Language in Sweden dating back to the 1960s (ibid.). In Finland, the first books and magazines in Easy Finnish were published in the early 1980s (Leskelä, 2021). Right now, Easy Language is well-established in Finland in practice, and the general attitude towards it is mainly positive (ibid.). Archives of *selkosuomi* [Easy Finnish] texts are available in the Language Bank of Finland (Kielipankki[1]). However, despite the availability of these resources, there seemingly has been no effort to create a sizeable aligned parallel corpus. Our research aims to fill this gap.

Our corpus is based on the Yle news archives available on Kielipankki (Yle Finnish News Archive 2019–2020[2] and Yle News Archive Easy-to-read Finnish 2019–2020[3]). Yle is a Finnish public service media company. It provides content for different audiences, including special target groups such as Easy Finnish language users. *Yle Uutiset selkosuomeksi* [Yle News in Easy Finnish] provides short (about 5 minutes) daily radio and TV broadcasts. The radio broadcasts are also published on Yle's website in text form. In this paper, our focus is on the news in text format.

The reason for creating this corpus is twofold. First, we wanted to provide a resource for studying the simplification strategies used by simple language content providers. This task requires parallel data in which Standard Finnish texts are aligned with their simplified versions. Second, we wanted to start working towards creating automatic text simplification tools for Finnish. Nowadays, automatic text simplification is typically seen

[1] https://www.kielipankki.fi/
[2] http://urn.fi/urn:nbn:fi:lb-2021050401
[3] http://urn.fi/urn:nbn:fi:lb-2021050701

Esplà-Gomis, Forcada, Kuzman, Ljubešić, van Noord, Ramírez-Sánchez, Tiedemann, Toral (eds.)
Proceedings of the 1st Workshop on Open Community-Driven Machine Translation, p. 21–26
Tampere, Finland, June 2023.

as a monolingual machine translation (MT) problem (Kriz et al., 2019), and MT models require parallel text data to train on. In this stage of our research, we have developed and applied the methodology for text alignment and manually assessed the alignments. The current dataset is available online and can be used for training models in low-resource settings. The Standard Finnish articles have 687555 words in total, and the Easy Finnish articles amount to 106733 words.

2 Related work

Parallel datasets for monolingual machine translation are often created based on news. For example, the CNN / DailyMail dataset (Hermann et al., 2015) of unique news articles written by journalists at CNN and the Daily Mail is used for abstractive and extractive summarization, and the ParaPhraserPlus corpus (Gudkov et al., 2020), which contains pairs of similar news headlines, is used for paraphrase generation. News-based corpora are also used for simplification, such as the Newsela corpus, which consists of news articles simplified manually by professional editors (Xu et al., 2015).

To align Easy Finnish articles with Standard Finnish equivalents, we used sentence embeddings. Multilingual sentence embeddings are often applied in paraphrase identification: for example, Girrbach (2022) showed that publicly available, pretrained models already achieve solid performance on this task. Khairova et al. (2022) also prove the advantages of using the fine-tuned Sentence-BERT language model for classifying paraphrased sentences over other modern models.

Current research on Easy Finnish covers many different resources and methods. One of the most recent papers containing corpus-based research focuses on the meanings of the word *ihminen* [human] and its usage in Easy Finnish and Standard Finnish news articles (Valtasalmi, 2021). It is a good example of research that could potentially benefit from our parallel corpus. Leskelä (2022) takes spoken Easy Finnish as a primary topic, and Hyppönen (2022) focuses on the cognitive accessibility assessment of different service websites.

According to the interviews conducted by Kulkki-Nieminen (2010), the main three target groups for news in Easy Finnish are immigrants, older adults, and people with intellectual disabilities. When *Yle Uutiset selkosuomeksi* started broadcasting, however, it was primarily aimed at heritage Finnish speakers who had learned Finnish at home but were no longer in the Finnish language environment (P. Seppä, personal communication, March 3, 2023). Kulkki-Nieminen (2010) conducted the interviews about the main topic of their research, namely the linguistic analysis of the language feature specific to Easy Finnish texts.

3 Dataset creation

3.1 Data selection and preprocessing

Kielipankki has multiple archives of Yle news. When we started creating our dataset, there was a more extensive archive comprising articles from 2011–2018 and a smaller archive for 2019–2020. To test our methodology and, at the same time, work with more modern texts, we chose the smaller archive.

Yle News in Easy Finnish and general Yle news, as well as the Swedish Yle partition, are stored in different archives. These archives are in JSON format and contain all available information about each article, including image captions within the text, topics, subjects, etc. Upon looking at the regular Finnish news archive, we noticed that Easy Finnish news articles are often mixed into it, so we had to filter out such occasions, removing entries with a "selkouutiset" topic. We did not perform additional preprocessing on the articles apart from cleaning out noise (non-Latin symbols, emojis, etc.).

3.2 Reducing the search space

There is no explicit alignment between the Easy Finnish news. Before looking for pairs of texts, we had to decide to only look for pairs between articles that came out on the same day. As we learned later, it is a valid approach since most regular news articles, if selected for Easy Finnish news, are translated and come on air within 24 hours (P. Seppä, personal communication, March 3, 2023). However, in some cases, non-urgent matters are covered in Easy Finnish news later.

The Easy Finnish news from each day's radio broadcast is usually combined on one page, and each paragraph covers its own event. Therefore, we matched these paragraphs to Standard Finnish news from the same day. Since we were looking for Standard Finnish equivalents of *selkosuomi* news in a one-to-all fashion, meaning that we looked through all Standard Finnish articles each time in order to find a match for a single *selkosuomi* article, we wanted to limit the number of Standard Finnish articles we have to look through at each step. Therefore, we did not just limit matching to articles from the same day but also only looked at Standard Finnish articles with some of the same subjects that the *selkosuomi* articles from this day had. Sometimes the articles are translated into Easy Finnish from Swedish (P. Seppä, personal communication, March 3, 2023), but for this project, we limited ourselves to matching only Finnish articles.

3.3 Alignment strategies

After the article matching explained in the previous section, we tried different techniques to find pairs of Finnish and Easy Finnish articles discussing the same topic.

The first strategy we tested was to try and match some articles based on the same image captions. For that, we lifted the same-day limitation. Unfortunately, upon inspection, this strategy proved to be unreliable, so we did not use it. Some captions were too broad to guarantee that all articles in which the corresponding image is found are on the same topic. However, we do not completely abandon this strategy and acknowledge that paired with paraphrase identification techniques, it could be used for expanding the dataset.

In order to find pairs of equivalent articles, we needed a tool to estimate the similarity between two texts. To do so, we looked at Doc2Vec and Sentence Transformers to obtain document embeddings that can be used to measure the cosine similarity between them.

Doc2Vec is a model that can represent a document (i.e., a text of one or more sentences) as a single vector. We used the Gensim implementation[4] based on Le and Mikolov (2014) and a SentencePiece[5] unigram language model (Kudo, 2018) for tokenization. To train the SentencePiece and Doc2Vec models, we used the Yle News archives from 2016–2018,[6] something not yet included in our dataset. A total of 202,656 articles were used for Doc2Vec, and 1 million randomly selected sentences for SentencePiece.

Sentence Transformers are language models used to derive semantically meaningful sentence embeddings. For this project, we used one of the models from SBERT[7] (Reimers and Gurevych, 2019): the multilingual knowledge-distilled version of multilingual Universal Sentence Encoder (Yang et al., 2020), version 2 (distiluse-base-multilingual-cased-v2). Version 1 is said to have better performance but does not include Finnish, so we opted for the second version. In order to get an embedding of a document, we take the average of all sentence vectors in the document. Since this model makes a vector for each individual sentence, transforming larger articles into vectors can be computationally expensive, so we only use the first 15 sentences to make an article's vector. It should be noted that the length of most Easy Finnish articles does not exceed this limit.

We manually compared both approaches on a set of Standard Finnish and Easy Finnish articles from the same random date. After looking at a sample of Standard and Easy Finnish articles from a few days, we found out that, even though the Sentence Transformer operated with only the first 15 sentences of the documents, as opposed to Doc2Vec, which utilized the entire documents, the Sentence Transformer performed better in finding equivalent articles. It also gave more representative scores: true pairs received high similarity scores (> 0.6), and false pairs received low scores (≤ 0.3), as opposed to the Doc2Vec model, where the scores were between 0.47 and 0.6. It is possible that a larger Doc2Vec model could have given better results. Still, for the sake of convenience and reproducibility of our work, we chose to proceed with the Sentence Transformer architecture for measuring semantic similarity.

3.4 Similarity threshold

For each Easy Finnish article in our collection, we found a Standard Finnish pair by choosing the article with the highest cosine similarity. Sometimes, it was impossible to find a good match. We had to establish a threshold of cosine similarity because, obviously, lower scores indicate a higher possibility of a false match. As seen in Figure 1, most pairs have cosine similarity scores between 0.6 and 0.7, with a little less than 500 pairs having a score of 0.5. We decided to perform the human evaluation on articles with scores from 0.6 to 1 to assess whether the scores actually represent semantic similarity and, if so, what the threshold should be.

[4]https://radimrehurek.com/gensim/models/doc2vec.html
[5]https://github.com/google/sentencepiece
[6]http://urn.fi/urn:nbn:fi:lb-2017070501
[7]https://www.sbert.net/

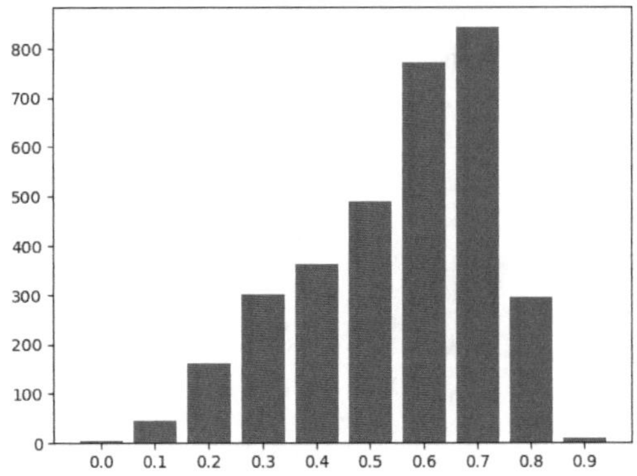

Figure 1: Distribution of cosine similarity scores across article pairs. X-axis is the approximated cosine similarity, y-axis is the number of pairs.

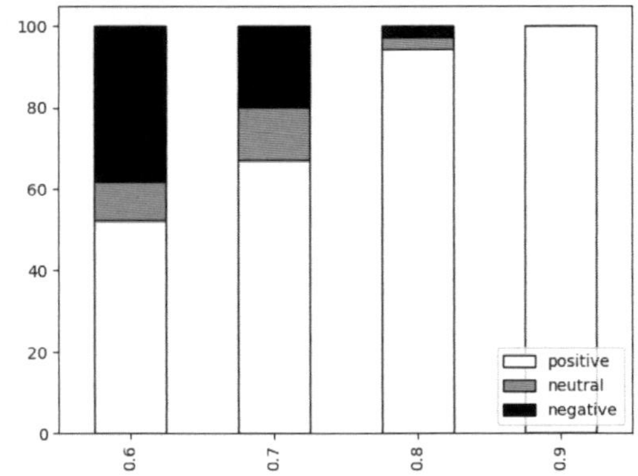

Figure 2: Percentages of labels given by the expert. X-axis is the approximated cosine similarity, y-axis is the percentage.

4 Evaluation

We ended up with 1919 pairs of articles with high (≥ 0.6) similarity scores. An expert was asked to evaluate each pair and give it one of three scores: "positive" – if the articles are definitely about the same topic, "negative" – if the articles definitely talk about different topics, or "neutral" – if it cannot be definitively said whether or not the articles talk about the same topic. The expert also gave comments on most of the negative cases. As seen in Figure 2, the percentage of negative labels grows with the decline of the similarity score. Therefore, we conclude that the cosine similarity indeed represents the semantic similarity of texts as seen by a human expert, and since the percentage of positive texts with labels between 0.6 and 0.7 is approx. 52%, there is no need to decrease the lower similarity threshold. There are 1257 "positive", 470 "negative", and 192 "neutral" article pairs in the dataset. Therefore, 65.5% of the data is "positive", 24.5% is "negative", and 10% is "neutral". These assessments can be used for classifying article pairs automatically, allowing for the creation of larger parallel datasets from the remaining Yle news archives.

The most common reasons for giving a pair of articles a "negative" or "neutral" score were as such:

- Easy Finnish article is about a completely different topic.
- Easy Finnish article covers a similar topic but does not exactly match the original article for various reasons (e.g., time, location, different focus).
- Easy Finnish article cannot be mapped to one original article but compiles information from several original articles.

It should be noted that some topics like Brexit, coronavirus, or weather forecasts were challenging to evaluate, especially when no particular time markers were mentioned. Due to the number of news on the same topic being too high, it was sometimes difficult to establish if two similar articles were definitely talking about the same event. There were also cases when the Easy Finnish article covered a topic relevant to the entire country of Finland, but the Standard Finnish article was limited only to one particular region (e.g., Lapland).

During the assessment, the expert compared the simplification strategies they saw in the Easy Finnish articles to the Easy Finnish Indicator/Selkomittari 2.0.[8] Selkomittari is a document that outlines the criteria for assessing how simple the text is. However, we did not use it to determine the quality of simplification but to see which strategies Easy Language content authors use in their work. According to the expert, the following characteristics are present in most of the simplified articles:

- The text mainly contains general vocabulary evaluated as familiar to the readers.
- The text does not contain lots of long words.
- The text contains no figures of speech that require creative reasoning to understand (to chip away at something, brain drain, etc.).

[8] `https://selkokeskus.fi/wp-content/uploads/2022/04/Selkokielen-mittari-2.0.pdf`

index in selko	index in regular	selko text	regular text	cos_sim	status	comments
3-10973979_0	3-10972641	Raakaöljyn hinta on noussut tänään melkein 10 prosenttia. Hinnannousun syy ovat Saudi-Arabiaan lauantaina tehdyt iskut...	Öljyn hinta nousi enemmän kuin Iranin vallankumouksen tai Kuwaitin sodan alettua. Öljyn hinta lähti odotetusti jyrkkään nousuun markkinoiden avauduttua maanantaiaamuna...	0,84402	Positive	Small difference in selkonews: last sentence

Table 1: An example of a dataset entry. The "index in selko" column includes the index of the entire entry in the Kielipankki dataset and the paragraph number after the underscore. Copyright: Yleisradio Oy, Finnish Broadcasting Company (Yle).

- The text contains high, precise numerical figures only if this is justified by its topic. If necessary, figures are approximated.
- Figures, numbers, units of measure, and relationships between numbers are presented visually.
- The text contains no abbreviations or acronyms, except for established ones which are better recognized as abbreviations than if written out in full (PDF, DVD).
- The text does not contain many language structures rated difficult.
- Clauses and sentences are mainly short.
- The text contains no words that have several different elements, such as derivative affixes, inflectional suffixes, and clitics.
- Sentence structures are simple. For the most part, they only have one subordinate clause.

It should be noted that in some cases, the vocabulary of Easy Finnish articles was not easy. For example, the expert has encountered the word *amurinleopardikissapariskunta* (the pair of Amur leopards), which was not used even in the original news article. Other cases of not-so-easy linguistic constructions found by the expert include complex sentence structures (in one case, a long sentence with four subordinate clauses) and colloquialisms without any additional comments on their meaning. There were also Easy Finnish articles that just summarized the original ones with no sentence-level simplification.

Obviously, not everything needs to be simplified. Sometimes, the authors of Easy Finnish texts will use complex words or constructions if they consider it necessary based on their expertise. The only reason we need to point out that sometimes the Easy Finnish articles might have "difficult" sentences is for other researchers to be aware of such cases. For example, suppose someone wants to make a sentence-aligned dataset based on Standard and Easy Finnish news to train an automatic text simplification model on. In that case, filtering out the not-so-easy Easy Finnish sentences may be beneficial before training.

5 Conclusions

We have described the creation of a parallel Finnish–Easy Finnish dataset based on news articles. With the help of a human assessor, we evaluated the automatically aligned pairs of articles, which helped us to determine the optimal similarity threshold and identify various cases of incorrect or ambiguous alignments. We also describe some of the simplification strategies used by authors during the creation of Easy Finnish articles.

This resource is now available for download on Kielipankki under the CLARIN ACA – NC license: `http://urn.fi/urn:nbn:fi:lb-2022111625`. The dataset can be used to study the linguistic properties of simplified Finnish and for various natural language processing applications. For example, it can be used for low-resource simplification or summarization. An example dataset entry can be seen in Table 1.

Some steps can be taken to improve our data collection procedures further. For example, a valuable contribution would be to find a way to match Easy Finnish articles to Swedish sources or Standard Finnish ones from different dates without it being too computationally expensive. Currently, we are working on extending the dataset and adding sentence-to-sentence alignments to create a more extensive dataset suitable for text simplification.

Acknowledgements: Anna Dmitrieva's work on this paper was partially supported by the Finnish Cultural Foundation (Grant №00230286).

References

Girrbach, Leander. 2022. PAR-MEX shared task submission description: Identifying Spanish paraphrases using pretrained models and translations. In *Proceedings of the Iberian Languages Evaluation Forum (IberLEF 2022)*.

Gudkov, Vadim, Olga Mitrofanova, and Elizaveta Filippskikh. 2020. Automatically ranked Russian paraphrase corpus for text generation. In *Proceedings of the Fourth Workshop on Neural Generation and Translation*, pages 54–59, Online, July. Association for Computational Linguistics.

Hermann, Karl Moritz, Tomas Kocisky, Edward Grefenstette, Lasse Espeholt, Will Kay, Mustafa Suleyman, and Phil Blunsom. 2015. Teaching machines to read and comprehend. In Cortes, C., N. Lawrence, D. Lee, M. Sugiyama, and R. Garnett, editors, *Advances in Neural Information Processing Systems*, volume 28. Curran Associates, Inc.

Hyppönen, Annikki. 2022. "Hyvä saavutettavuus hyödyttää kaikkia" - Kognitiivisen saavutettavuusarvioinnin käytänteitä [Good accessibility benefits everyone: cognitive accessibility assessment practices]. In H. Katajamäki, M. Enell-Nilsson, H. Kauppinen-Räisänen H. Limatius, editor, *Responsible Communication*, volume 14, pages 43–59.

Khairova, Nina, Anastasiia Shapovalova, Orken Mamyrbayev, Nataliia Sharonova, and Kuralay Mukhsina. 2022. Using BERT model to identify sentences paraphrase in the news corpus. In *Proceedings of the 6th International Conference on Computational Linguistics and Intelligent Systems (COLINS 2022). Volume I: Main Conference*, volume 3171, pages 38–48.

Kriz, Reno, Joao Sedoc, Marianna Apidianaki, Carolina Zheng, Gaurav Kumar, Eleni Miltsakaki, and Chris Callison-Burch. 2019. Complexity-weighted loss and diverse reranking for sentence simplification. In *Proceedings of NAACL-HLT*, pages 3137–3147.

Kudo, Taku. 2018. Subword Regularization: Improving Neural Network Translation Models with Multiple Subword Candidates. In *Proceedings of the 56th Annual Meeting of the Association for Computational Linguistics (Volume 1: Long Papers)*, pages 66–75, Melbourne, Australia, July. Association for Computational Linguistics.

Kulkki-Nieminen, Auli. 2010. *Selkoistettu uutinen. Lingvistinen analyysi selkotekstin erityispiirteistä [Simplified news article. Linguistic analysis of special features of Easy Language text]*. Ph.D. thesis.

Le, Quoc and Tomas Mikolov. 2014. Distributed Representations of Sentences and Documents. In Xing, Eric P. and Tony Jebara, editors, *Proceedings of the 31st International Conference on Machine Learning*, volume 32 of *Proceedings of Machine Learning Research*, pages 1188–1196, Bejing, China, 22–24 Jun. PMLR.

Leskelä, Leealaura. 2021. Easy language in Finland. In Camilla Lindholm, Ulla Vanhatalo, editor, *Handbook of Easy Languages in Europe*, volume 8 of *Easy – Plain – Accessible*, pages 149–190. Frank & Timme, 1 edition.

Leskelä, Leealaura. 2022. *Selkopuhetta!: Puhuttu selkokieli kehitysvammaisten henkilöiden ja ammattilaisten vuorovaikutuksessa [Speak Easy Language! Spoken Easy Language in interactions between persons with intellectual disabilities and professionals]*. Ph.D. thesis.

Lindholm, Camilla and Ulla Vanhatalo. 2021. Introduction. In Camilla Lindholm, Ulla Vanhatalo, editor, *Handbook of Easy Languages in Europe*, volume 8 of *Easy – Plain – Accessible*, pages 11–26. Frank & Timme, 1 edition.

Maaß, Christiane. 2020. *Easy Language – Plain Language – Easy Language Plus*, volume 3 of *Easy – Plain – Accessible*. Frank & Timme, 1 edition.

Reimers, Nils and Iryna Gurevych. 2019. Sentence-BERT: Sentence embeddings using Siamese BERT-networks. In *Proceedings of the 2019 Conference on Empirical Methods in Natural Language Processing and the 9th International Joint Conference on Natural Language Processing (EMNLP-IJCNLP)*, pages 3982–3992, Hong Kong, China, November. Association for Computational Linguistics.

Valtasalmi, Idastiina. 2021. Selkoa ihmisestä: Ihminen-sanan merkitykset ja käyttö selkokielisissä sanomalehtiteksteissä [Easy about a human: Human-word meanings and usage in Easy Language news articles]. *Sananjalka*, 63, March.

Xu, Wei, Chris Callison-Burch, and Courtney Napoles. 2015. Problems in current text simplification research: New data can help. *Transactions of the Association for Computational Linguistics*, 3:283–297.

Yang, Yinfei, Daniel Cer, Amin Ahmad, Mandy Guo, Jax Law, Noah Constant, Gustavo Hernandez Abrego, Steve Yuan, Chris Tar, Yun-hsuan Sung, Brian Strope, and Ray Kurzweil. 2020. Multilingual universal sentence encoder for semantic retrieval. In *Proceedings of the 58th Annual Meeting of the Association for Computational Linguistics: System Demonstrations*, pages 87–94, Online, July. Association for Computational Linguistics.

Extended abstracts

A Python Tool for Selecting Domain-Specific Data in Machine Translation

Javad Pourmostafa Roshan Sharami, Dimitar Shterionov, and Pieter Spronck
Department of Cognitive Science and Artificial Intelligence, Tilburg University, Tilburg, The Netherlands
{j.pourmostafa,d.shterionov,p.spronck}@tilburguniversity.edu

1 Introduction

As the volume of data for Machine Translation (MT) grows, the need for models that can perform well in specific use cases, like patent and medical translations, becomes increasingly important. Unfortunately, generic models do not work well in such cases, as they often fail to handle domain-specific style and terminology. Only using datasets that cover domains similar to the target domain to train MT systems can effectively lead to high translation quality (for a domain-specific use-case) (Wang et al., 2017; Pourmostafa Roshan Sharami et al., 2021; Pourmostafa Roshan Sharami et al., 2022). This highlights the limitation of data-driven MT when trained on general-domain data, regardless of dataset size.

To address this challenge, researchers have implemented various strategies to improve domain-specific translation using Domain Adaptation (DA) methods (Saunders, 2022; Sharami et al., 2023). The DA process involves initially training a generic model, which is then fine-tuned using a domain-specific dataset (Chu and Wang, 2018). One approach to generating a domain-specific dataset is to select similar data from generic corpora for a specific language pair, and then utilize both general (to train) and domain-specific (to fine-tune) parallel corpora for MT. In line with this approach, we developed *a language-agnostic Python tool implementing the methodology proposed by Sharami et al. (2022).* This tool uses monolingual domain-specific corpora to generate a parallel in-domain corpus, facilitating data selection for DA.

The tool's operation requires three inputs: (i) a parallel generic corpus for the source language, (ii) a parallel generic corpus for the target language (iii) a monolingual domain-specific corpus for the source language. Additionally, users can input their desired number of selected data as an optional parameter. Once these inputs are provided, the pre-trained S-BERT (Reimers and Gurevych, 2019) model is employed to transform inputs (i) and (iii) using Siamese and triplet networks. We reduced the original word embedding dimension from 768 to 32 using PCA (Jolliffe, 2011) to make it less computationally expensive. If the size of the corpus (iii) is exceeded by the desired number of selected data, the generic corpora are split into multiple equal parts, and each of these parts is used separately in the subsequent step.

The final step involves using semantic search to find generic sentences that are similar to domain-specific data. This is done by comparing the vectors of sentences and ranking them based on their cosine similarity score. The sentence with the highest similarity score is labeled as Top 1, while the one with the lowest similarity score is labeled as Top N. The default value for N is 5, which is based on the original research paper, but users can choose a different value for N. For each split, the tool then creates a CSV file that includes information about the domain-specific sentence (labeled as `Query`), the top selected source and target sentences (labeled as $topN_{src}$ and $topN_{trg}$), and their corresponding similarity scores. By concatenating the CSV columns generated, one can obtain as much data as previously requested.

Our tool is particularly useful to the MT community as it addresses the scarcity of parallel domain-specific data across different language pairs. By using our tool, users can seamlessly select domain-specific data from generic corpora to train a domain-specific MT model. This tool is typically used when there is a lack of domain-specific data or when only monolingual data is available. However, our tool is generic and not limited to the size of the domain-specific data.

Our tool is licensed under the MIT License and is accessible to the public for free at `https://github.com/JoyeBright/DataSelection-NMT/tree/main/Tools_DS`.

Esplà-Gomis, Forcada, Kuzman, Ljubešić, van Noord, Ramírez-Sánchez, Tiedemann, Toral (eds.)
Proceedings of the 1st Workshop on Open Community-Driven Machine Translation, p. 29–30
Tampere, Finland, June 2023.

References

Chu, Chenhui and Rui Wang. 2018. A survey of domain adaptation for neural machine translation. In *Proceedings of the 27th International Conference on Computational Linguistics*, pages 1304–1319, Santa Fe, New Mexico, USA, August. Association for Computational Linguistics.

Jolliffe, Ian, 2011. *Principal Component Analysis*, pages 1094–1096. Springer Berlin Heidelberg, Berlin, Heidelberg.

Pourmostafa Roshan Sharami, Javad, Dimitar Shterionov, and Pieter Spronck. 2021. A novel pipeline for domain detection and selecting in-domain sentences in machine translation systems. In *The 31st Meeting of Computational Linguistics in The Netherlands (CLIN 31)*.

Pourmostafa Roshan Sharami, Javad, Elena Murgolo, and Dimitar Shterionov. 2022. Quality estimation for the translation industry – data challenges. June. The 32nd Meeting of Computational Linguistics in The Netherlands, CLIN ; Conference date: 17-06-2022 Through 17-06-2022.

Reimers, Nils and Iryna Gurevych. 2019. Sentence-BERT: Sentence embeddings using Siamese BERT-networks. In *Proceedings of the 2019 Conference on Empirical Methods in Natural Language Processing and the 9th International Joint Conference on Natural Language Processing (EMNLP-IJCNLP)*, pages 3982–3992, Hong Kong, China, November. Association for Computational Linguistics.

Saunders, Danielle. 2022. Domain adaptation and multi-domain adaptation for neural machine translation: A survey. *Journal of Artificial Intelligence Research*, 75:351–424.

Sharami, Javad Pourmostafa Roshan, Dimitar Shterionov, and Pieter Spronck. 2022. Selecting parallel in-domain sentences for neural machine translation using monolingual texts.

Sharami, Javad Pourmostafa Roshan, Dimitar Shterionov, Frédéric Blain, Eva Vanmassenhove, Mirella De Sisto, Chris Emmery, and Pieter Spronck. 2023. Tailoring domain adaptation for machine translation quality estimation.

Wang, Rui, Andrew Finch, Masao Utiyama, and Eiichiro Sumita. 2017. Sentence embedding for neural machine translation domain adaptation. In *Proceedings of the 55th Annual Meeting of the Association for Computational Linguistics (Volume 2: Short Papers)*, pages 560–566, Vancouver, Canada, July. Association for Computational Linguistics.

MutNMT, an open-source NMT tool for educational purposes

Gema Ramírez Sánchez
Prompsit Language Engineering, S.L.
gramirez@prompsit.com

We present MutNMT,[1] an open-source web application for educational purposes to introduce non-experts to NMT. The tool, developed within the MultiTraiNMT project[2] along with other training materials (a book[3] and activities[4]), gathers the feedback of academic and industrial project partners and also external collaborators.

MutNMT is based on open-source code from JoeyNMT (Kreutzer et al., 2019),[5] an open-source minimalist neural machine translation toolkit also for educational purposes. It uses its Transformer architecture to train NMT models. A new feature to extract the n-best list of translation candidates was contributed to JoeyNMT from MutNMT.

MutNMT provides a user-friendly interface to manage the full process of building an NMT system, provided that training data is available, through different sections: 1) data set uploader and library for own and shared data sets, 2) engines library providing access to own or shared models, their details and a full training log, 3) training section where users can select corpora and set training parameters, 4) translation section for short texts and documents, 5) model inspection and comparison among models section, 6) evaluation with automatic metrics and, finally 7) administration of users and monitoring of processes and server.

The tool was conceived for an educational environment with very limited computational capabilities, e.g. a server with 2-4 GPUs. There are 3 different roles: beginners (not allowed to train), experts (allowed to train) and administrators. To train a new model, 1-hour training slots are allocated and can be resumed for an additional hour slot. To provide a good experience to users, optimal ranges for data sizes and training parameters were estimated. Training sets are limited to 500k sentence pairs, and development and test sets to 5k. Customisable parameters as vocabulary, beam or batch size, validation frequency, stopping condition and duration are also constrained.

An engaged community of users is starting to arise around MutNMT. Some instances have been deployed successfully in different universities and are being actively used to train students and professional translators. The MultiTraiNMT project official instance provided by the Universitat Autònoma de Barcelona[6] currently has 560 users from a variety of companies and research institutions mainly related to translation technology training. Access only requires a Google account or no requirement for the demo version. Further development plans include new roles for research-oriented experiments with more flexible training time and data sizes, API usage, usage integrated with CAT-tools and further evaluation metrics.

References

Kreutzer, Julia, Jasmijn Bastings, and Stefan Riezler. 2019. Joey NMT: A minimalist NMT toolkit for novices. In *Proceedings of the 2019 Conference on Empirical Methods in Natural Language Processing and the 9th International Joint Conference on Natural Language Processing (EMNLP-IJCNLP): System Demonstrations*, pages 109–114, Hong Kong, China, November. Association for Computational Linguistics.

[1]https://github.com/Prompsit/mutnmt
[2]https://www.multitrainmt.eu/index.php/
[3]Machine translation for everyone: Empowering users in the age of artificial intelligence https://langsci-press.org/catalog/book/342
[4]https://github.com/jaspock/mt4everyone
[5]https://github.com/joeynmt/joeynmt
[6]https://ntradumatica.uab.cat/

Association for Computational Linguistics
209 N. Eighth Street
Stroudsburg, Pennsylvania 18360

ISBN 978-1-7138-8995-3

9 781713 889953

CURRAN ASSOCIATES INC.
proceedings.com

22nd Chinese National Conference on Computational Linguistic (CCL 2023)

Tutorial Abstracts

Harbin, China
3 - 5 August 2023